This book belongs to

USE
ME

Good morning

Good night

Please

Thank you

Sorry

Welcome

Bye

Early to bed early to rise...

Make your own bed.

Brush your teeth twice daily.

Wash your hands before eating.

Bathe every day

Keep your hair tidy.

Do not talk while eating.
Do not stuff your mouth while eating.

Do not waste food.

Do not stretch across the table. Ask someone to pass what you need.

Be punctual as time is precious.

Take proper care of your books.

Greet every teacher

Do not waste time when you ought to study.

Throw your garbage in a bin.

Obey traffic rules

Do not litter

Do not shout

Be patient

Do not disturb anyone who is doing his/her work.

Do not disturb an animal while it is sleeping or eating.

Obey the rules of the game you play.

Do not hit anyone.

Be polite when relatives and guests visit. Wish them properly.

Never pick your nose in public.